*The World We Once
Lived In*

The World We Once Lived In

WANGARI MAATHAI

PENGUIN BOOKS — GREEN IDEAS

PENGUIN BOOKS

UK | USA | Canada | Ireland | Australia
India | New Zealand | South Africa

Penguin Books is part of the Penguin Random House group of companies
whose addresses can be found at global.penguinranomhouse.com.

First published in the United States by Doubleday Religion, an imprint of the
Crown Publishing Group, a division of Random House, Inc., New York. 2010
This selection published in Penguin Books 2021

001

Text copyright © Wangari Muta Maathai, 2010

Set in 12.5/15pt Dante MT Std
Typeset by Jouve (UK), Milton Keynes
Printed and bound in Great Britain by Clays Ltd, Elcograf S.p.A.

The authorized representative in the EEA is Penguin Random House Ireland,
Morrison Chambers, 32 Nassau Street, Dublin D02 YH68

A CIP catalogue record for this book is available from the British Library

ISBN: 978–0–141–99693–6

www.greenpenguin.co.uk

Contents

Behold my works! See how beautiful they are, how excellent! All that I have created for your sake did I create it. See to it that you do not spoil and destroy my world; for if you do, there will be no one to repair it after you.

– Ecclesiastes Rabbah 7:13

For my granddaughter, Ruth Wangari

The Wounds

In early 2009, I joined a small group of concerned individuals, a government minister, and members of the press on a fact-finding visit to a program run by a timber company active in the Republic of the Congo to ascertain whether it was a model of what could be called sustainable forestry management.

Four years earlier, in 2005, the ten countries that contain parts of the Congo Basin rain forest in central Africa had invited me to be the ecosystem's goodwill ambassador. The Congo Basin is an area of 700,000 square miles, some fifty million people, and tens of thousands of species of flora and fauna. My responsibility would be to help raise the profile of the region: its biodiversity and the significant role it is believed to play in regulating the planet's climate. I readily agreed, since I'd seen for myself how vital forests were to human communities and other forms of life that dwell in them.

Scientists call the Congo Basin's forest the world's 'second lung,' after the Amazon, because of the sheer volume of carbon dioxide it absorbs and the oxygen it exhales. Keeping this ecosystem healthy and using the resources it contains in a manner that's both sustainable and equitable without destroying it are not merely of concern for central Africa, but for the continent at large. Without the Congo forest, Africa would be one huge desert. It needs to be protected.

Our small group caught a plane from the Republic of the Congo's capital, Brazzaville, and flew for hours north and then east, over mile upon mile of dense greenery. We arrived at a landing strip in Pokola, a small town not far from the border with Cameroon. A representative of the timber company met us and explained that they'd been harvesting trees in the region for more than twenty years. He pointed to an area that had been logged about a decade earlier. I could see by the amount of vegetation and the number and height of the trees that, at least in this one segment, the forest had been able to regenerate itself.

From there, the group boarded two boats and traveled up the Sangha, a tributary of the vast Congo River. The Sangha was wider than an average four-lane street in any city, with dark, clear, placid waters that meandered silently through the forest. When I was a child, the streams where I grew up in Kenya's Central Highlands were narrow, fast moving, and clear. The water made a whooshing noise as it hurtled over the stones of the riverbed. However, too often these days, deforestation has caused siltation of many rivers, and the waters themselves have become so shallow they barely whisper over the pebbles. Indeed, sometimes the beds dry out altogether. The Sangha was a stark contrast, and a pleasant one – broad, unmuddied, and full of water.

After about an hour on the river, we came to an opening in the forest where we alighted from the boat. We were greeted by local residents, including Aka pygmies, who live in the forest, and others from Bantu communities (a group of peoples in east and southern Africa related by language that comprise the majority of the continent's population). As the people clapped and sang in welcome, I joined them to express my appreciation and gratitude, even though I didn't understand their words. What required no translator, however, was the evidence that in spite of the joy on their faces these people were very poor. Their clothes were in tatters, and their drawn faces and thin bodies showed signs of a hard life in the forest.

Our host, the timber company representative, wanting to demonstrate the aspects of the business that were socially and environmentally responsible, took us to a site where the company had, he said, worked with the Aka to protect trees important to their culture or for food. While I was pleased to see this sensitivity, the area of forest being saved was small compared to the area being logged. However, the local community appeared happy with the effort to conserve trees that were important to their culture and lifestyle.

The company was also anxious to show us how their workers felled trees selectively and sustainably. We were given crash helmets, and then turned our attention to a large sapele tree, about seventy feet tall and perhaps eight feet in diameter, with roots that fanned out from the base and anchored themselves firmly in the ground. The canopy of the tree was broad, shaped like an umbrella, and filled with smallish, dark green leaves.

An overseer instructed ten or so men with chain saws to cut it so it fell in a particular direction and didn't crush other, younger trees that were growing. This concern for the other trees also impressed me. For ten or fifteen minutes we watched as the men sawed. Finally, the tree swayed and fell to the ground with a huge bang that seemed to reverberate across the entire forest.

Our host told us that the tree almost certainly had been more than two centuries old. Two hundred years! I thought. For all we knew, it might have survived for another two centuries: retaining water and anchoring soil throughout its root system, storing carbon and releasing oxygen, and providing a home for birds, numerous insects, beetles, and other species in its trunk and canopy. Certainly, the fact that it had taken saws several minutes to bring the sapele to the ground showed that it was not ready to come down, not ready to loosen its tenacious grip on the soil, and not ready to stop providing environmental services.

As I watched the tree fall, tears welled in my eyes. The timber company representative noticed that I had become emotional. 'Don't worry,' he said. 'There are millions of other trees out there in the forest.'

This seemed small comfort. As we walked back to where we'd embarked, I asked the representative how much of the sapele would become timber. Thirty-five percent was the reply. I was surprised at how little that was, and inquired why the other 65 percent wasn't processed and shipped overseas, or transported to Brazzaville, Kinshasa, or even Nairobi, cities where it would be valuable and much sought after. Our host answered that this wasn't logistically possible or financially viable. Besides, he added, unless other logging companies operating in the Congo were required to process and export more or all of the trees they cut, his company's importation and use of the needed technology would put it at a financial disadvantage. Nevertheless, for the sake of the environment the company was planning to begin using this technology within the next three years. How would they do it competitively?

I didn't have to wait long to find out what happened to the 65 percent of the sapele. Our group was taken to another site, where Vietnamese workers were feeding the remainder of the tree into a hot kiln where bricks were being made. Those bricks would be used to build houses nearby for the timber company's workers. The local people took the rest of the wood and turned it into charcoal, which was used as fuel both locally and in distant towns and cities. Thick smoke and ash blanketed the area. I felt it in my throat and eyes.

What I saw that day felt like a wound on many levels. What stung me most was the waste involved in the transformation of that two-hundred-year-old sapele. Instead of turning the tree into fodder for the kiln, the timber company could have constructed their workers' houses from the lumber itself. The local people didn't use bricks to construct their homes, nor did they have the knowledge or technology to make bricks. Workers from abroad had to come to the Congo to do the work instead. Bricks, of course, aren't essential for dwellings. But homes made from them are seen as modern and progressive in much of Africa, and thus are desired. (Most Africans don't know that houses built of wood in developed countries have stood for hundreds of years.) The company had obviously conceded to public opinion and decided that its workers wouldn't live in wood houses, or those constructed of more traditional materials such as mud and straw. They would build brick houses even if they had to import experts from Vietnam to do so.

There was another bitter irony here. As the

kiln devoured the sapele, it spewed into the air carbon dioxide, one of the main gases causing global warming, which an intact Congo forest helps slow. Yet in the context created by that logging operation, using the majority of the wood provided by an ancient tree as kindling and charcoal was deemed both efficient and accepted practice. How much of the Congo forest would, I wondered, become charcoal and ashes?

As the remains of the once living, vibrant tree were being turned into burnt, dead matter, the smoke, combined with the red glare of embers in the kiln, seemed to me a more-than-adequate definition of hell – and not just because smoke, soot, and red flame are the standard motifs the Christian tradition has assigned to it. It was hell because of the environmental destruction, poverty, and desperate scrambling around for resources that goes along with the burning of charcoal. It was hell because of the dehumanization that occurs when people search for riches in the mud and disease of pits and mines and mercury-tainted rivers. It was hell because the burning of wood for charcoal is a method for acquiring energy that only increases the chances of more desperation and degradation later on as wood becomes scarcer, the climate dries out, desertification intensifies, and the atmosphere and water sources are polluted or desiccated, and eventually disappear.

It is worth noting that this operation was run by a responsible company: one sensitive to the cultural and spiritual practices of the forest-dwelling Aka; concerned that when trees were cut, others weren't harmed; and committed to regenerating the forest where it had logged the trees. This was a company doing what it could to manage its section of the Congo forest sustainably.

The company was also providing jobs and income to the local people, as well as the government. It was demonstrating a commitment to a remote area of a country and region marked by political instability, massive poverty, and lack of economic opportunity. The company was also aware that timber companies from other countries were either operating in the region or waiting to take its place if it pulled out. Such companies could be less scrupulous and more destructive than this one.

When the company representative told me that millions of trees remained in the forest, he was right. The Congo forest is huge. No doubt, in time, another tree will grow in the place where the felled one once stood. But underlying our host's comment was a worldview that's all too common: that there are always more trees to be cut, more land to be utilized, more fish to be caught, more water to dam or tap, and more minerals to be mined or prospected for. It's this attitude toward the earth, that it has unlimited capacity, and the valuing of resources for what they can buy, not what they do, that has created so many of the deep ecological wounds visible across the world.

The destruction of the environment is driven by an insatiable craving for more.

The word 'craving,' so implicated in the physical exploitation of the environment, indicates psychological desperation and spiritual weakness.

It illustrates a want that goes beyond simply filling one's belly or satisfying one's thirst. I think of the Aka. The timber company in the Congo forest had tractors, trucks, boats, and chain saws that could bring down great trees in a matter of minutes, trees that had sustained the Aka in the forest, perhaps for centuries. These trees were being cut to supply timber for people far away whose tastes and desires had expanded to such an extent that they had created the capacity to infiltrate the thick forest and remove these resources. To the local people the forest was no longer a blessing but rather a curse. Their future generations would not be able to follow the streams, gather fruits and berries, hunt, and be sustained by the forests – that is, if we let them vanish.

The Source had placed the Aka in the middle of the forest, supplying them with enough knowledge and ingenuity to find roots and berries and leaves and wildlife to eat. It had provided them with the ability to domesticate a few animals, and had enabled them to bring into existence a local market where they could buy clothes. The Aka had traveled through the Congo and still the forest had stood: each tree a macrocosm with numerous ecosystems, and each tree a microcosm of the greater ecosystem around it, and then each ecosystem still further a component of the whole basin itself.

In this way, the Aka and the forest had managed to survive for centuries, perhaps thousands of years, without money or any of the pieces of furniture or commodities for which they were exchanging the natural resources. They had hunted the animals sustainably, but they were now helping to kill them in large numbers to supply the bush-meat market, which has the potential to empty the forests of wild fauna and endangered species, such as primates, that cannot be replenished.

In spite of the greater economic activity surrounding them, you could sense the *craving* among the Aka: a palpable feeling that they knew something more existed out there than what they were used to; a sense of dissatisfaction among these people that they were missing out. It was clear from their clothing and the signs of want that they were not comfortable, and were not sustaining themselves. A profound dissonance existed in the enormity of the gap between the different modes of knowledge and worldviews of the peoples concerned. It makes one wonder how it would be possible to balance such extremes with a policy that respected both the sustenance of what was left of the Aka's way of life and their environment, and the hunger the rest of the world has for what is contained in these forests. When the trees are gone, one might ask, will the cravings be satisfied? What will remain for the Aka? Indeed, what will be left of them, of who they are?

The challenge I face as the goodwill ambassador for the Congo Basin ecosystem is to straddle the divides between these different manifestations of craving: to persuade international agencies, governments, industries, peoples, and even the Aka standing on the shore to see the forest in a holistic way. The task must be to ensure that all stakeholders do not simply view the forest as a resource to be plundered but have enough compassion and respect to comprehend that not only do the Aka depend on it, so do millions of people in the countries of the entire Congo Basin, the whole of Africa, and indeed the global community.

As I write, the debate continues over how to meet the vast human needs in the countries of the Congo Basin while conserving its vast biological diversity. Development plans agreed upon by numerous countries in the region call on the governments to eradicate poverty and promise support to help them do so. But of course, many of these countries are simultaneously encouraged to exploit natural resources as a result of the insatiable demands of global trade rules, or the requirement to repay large national debts. So the exploitation of the environment continues. The paramount interest is economics and monetary value, which is why the spiritual values aren't present in the boardrooms where decisions on logging the Congo forests are made. Without these values, though, the resources are seen as something to exploit for profit, with far more value dead (as planking for a deck or hot tub or floor in developed countries) than alive, providing ecosystemic services that are, quite literally, priceless.

If these spiritual values were part of discussions about the forests, everyone, from corporations to politicians to the local communities, would look at these resources very differently. Through these values, we would develop an appreciation for the services those forests are providing not only for the Aka but as the world's 'second lung,' regulating the climate in Africa, China, the United States, Europe, and elsewhere. And we'd be grateful and work to protect the forests, even as we redoubled our commitment to ending the Aka's poverty.

Many people such as the Aka, who are very connected to the natural world, aren't necessarily connected by choice; close to the earth and directly reliant on its resources is where they happen to be. In the industrialized world, on the other hand, many people have become disconnected from nature. They may be equally dependent on natural resources, but the chain that connects them to the resources has many more links in it. They may have everything materially – everything the Aka don't have – but they still feel empty spiritually. They search for other forms of meaning or other ways of relating to the world. Some may visit traditional peoples like the Aka, looking for *their* truth; some will find ways that they, too, can reconnect to the earth, simply by being in nature. But sometimes those from industrialized nations don't find the answers among the indigenous peoples. For communities such as the Aka have their own ways of relating to the earth that may or may not be exportable. They may still be practicing the traditions of their ancestors, but may not be able to help explain that world to the seeker, who is trying to understand and recapture the world we *all* once lived in.

As the story in Numbers attests, the desire for more made the Israelites forget horrible experiences in Egypt such as slavery and imprisonment. At the same time, this desire itself can create intense suffering, by allowing us to disregard the past and not plan for the future. To be able to control that craving, to say, 'No more, enough is enough,' is a matter of monumental discipline. This will not occur unless it's linked to the raising of consciousness that is essential to healing the earth. People with this higher consciousness see the world with the right perspective. They value balance and harmony and are able to draw a line below or beyond that which they wouldn't go to to fulfill their cravings; these are among the people whose achievements we admire and whose actions inspire us.

In the industrialized regions, where people are mainly urban, overconsumption is the main craving and therefore the major ecological challenge. The wounds, though, are less visible, until one visits, for instance, a landfill or a smoggy city, or sees a polluted river with dead fish in it. In the poorer regions of the world, on the other hand, it's deprivation, due to persistent inequalities, that leads people to overexploit their local environment: to clear trees and vegetation, to cultivate crops on steep slopes or in forested areas, to induce massive soil erosion, or to overgraze their livestock and reduce pasture to near desert.

It wasn't always this way. Before the wealthy nations were as rich as they are today, thrift was a common value and older people often enjoined younger ones not to waste, whether it was fuel, food, material possessions, or their potential. The Kikuyus, for example, had many rituals and practices that expressed gratitude for the bounty of their region and its continuance. Traditionally, a small portion of the first harvest was always delivered to a specific open area or grove, away from the village and usually at a crossroad that everyone knew of. This was called the 'granary of God' (*ikĕutilde;mbĕitilde; ria Ngai*). Here, every farmer was obliged to leave a portion of what he had harvested as a kind of tithe for the wild animals or the very poor or those who, because of a physical or mental disability, weren't able to grow or harvest their own food. In this way, the community ensured not only that there would be enough to eat, but that those less fortunate, as well as wildlife, would also have access to food. It was their way of contributing to the common good.

In a similar vein, any member of the extended

family or group blessed with wealth, such as land or livestock, was obligated through custom to give the rights of cultivation to another less fortunate member of the community in genuine need of land. By providing labor to the benefactor, an individual could also earn livestock and graze them on the benefactor's land for a short time, until he could acquire his own land. Diligence and hard work were considered virtues and one did everything possible to become self-reliant and independent. Exploiting the benefactor or overextending one's stay was considered a vice, and the community exerted pressure on everyone to practice a responsible livelihood.

The Kikuyus also had a tradition of hospitality that included ensuring that no one should die of starvation while traveling through Kikuyu territory. While, of course, many travelers would have carried enough food with them to last the passage, sometimes they miscalculated the time or length of their journey, or were waylaid by bad weather or swollen rivers and thus ran short. Because of these realities, Kikuyus believed that travelers were permitted to eat food in the fields if they were hungry. Due to the fertility of the land then, the fields were full of sugarcane, sweet potatoes, and bananas (which, if not ripe, could be roasted to become edible). Significantly, however, one was only allowed to eat as much as one needed. Travelers could not carry the supply with them; that would be considered greedy and a sign of ingratitude. This custom had many impacts. First, it ensured that no one individual's land was denuded of crops, because there was a limit on how much a traveler could eat in a given period of time. And second, the remnants of the food not consumed by the traveler could be eaten by someone else or used to feed domestic or even wild animals. These two direct purposes encapsulated a third, more indirect, cultural message – that no one should be too greedy or take advantage of another's generosity. This sense of restraint was also considered a virtue.

What was taken from the fields was only what was needed and not what was desired. Waste was reduced, and as light as possible an ecological footprint was left on the land. It also offered the kind of food security that today so many in the poorer parts of the world lack. While self-reliance was essential (everyone who could cultivated food crops), the community embraced the value of service to travelers, of supporting others in times of need.

The Kikuyus did not have a particular spiritual reverence for animals apart, perhaps, from goats, which were sacrificed during various ceremonies. Nevertheless, they weren't ruthless in protecting their domesticated animals. The occasional loss of a goat to wild animals, or even the risk of hyenas eating the remains of the community's dead – who were either interred in shallow graves or even left unburied – was accepted as part of the cycle of life. Traditional Kikuyu houses also had an area inside where one's goats or sheep, especially the young and vulnerable, spent the night. Not only, of course, did this protect the animal from the elements and from being attacked by predators, but the animals kept the house warm and free of parasites such as the chigoe flea.

Because Kikuyus lived very close to their animals, they grew to know their idiosyncrasies and responded well to their needs. In an act that is still performed by millions of children in rural areas around the world, before I went to school as a child I would go into the field to check on my father's goats and sheep. When it came to killing their domestic animals, the Kikuyus had – like many traditional communities, and indeed Jewish and Muslim ritual slaughter – a set of social taboos that made it a weighty and consequential act. Permission to kill was sought from the Creator and the ancestors. To protect the animal from the trauma of instant death, it would first be denied air and blood to the brain before a knife touched its body.

Although these traditions were still alive during the early part of the twentieth century, they quickly died out as Christianity took hold. The new cash economy created by the colonial authority, quickly embraced by the locals, and continued by postcolonial governments encouraged natives to plant cash crops such as coffee, tea, and corn. Traditional foods were trivialized and considered only suitable for the poor and unsophisticated. Not only did this mean that there wasn't extra food for the casual traveler, but the farmers themselves now did not have adequate, nutritious food. With the money earned from cash crops, native Africans began buying food, rather than producing it. The traditional diet that was mostly vegetarian and full of fresh greens – with many varieties of bananas, and grains such as sorghum and millet – gave way to imported food crops eaten in industrialized countries, a diet dominated by fats and sugars, salt, and processed foods. Needless to say, diseases associated with eating and living this way overtook the local communities with a vengeance.

Goat culture and traditions that inculcated respect and a sense of gratitude for animals sacrificed to sustain human life were abandoned. Whereas Kikuyus traditionally had eaten meat on special days or as a condiment, the more affluent they became the more they adopted the practice of the new arrivals in trying never to go a day without animal flesh. Today, even the tourism industry has joined in by starting the very popular 'carnivore' restaurants, which originally featured wildlife meat. This development cultivated an appetite for bush meat that expanded to the locals. Indeed, the Kikuyus began to crave such a diet.

The craving for bush meat has meant an increase in poaching, as the animals' skins, horns, and now flesh have a price tag on them. The land on which these animals used to roam free has been commercialized, fenced in, and privatized. In much the same way as traditional human communities are confined in their reservations, so wildlife is now enclosed in ever-diminishing parks and wilderness.

On a worldwide scale, the ravenous craving for more has very direct consequences on our environment. A 2006 study by the United Nations Food and Agriculture Organization, for example, found that the planet's livestock sector, responsible for the production and delivery of meat and dairy products, is also responsible for approximately 18 percent of global greenhouse gas emissions.

This is more than the total for all forms of transportation combined and nearly on par with the greenhouse gas toll of deforestation and forest degradation. Intensive animal agriculture, and its massive requirements for feed for farmed animals, is also polluting air, water, and land around the globe, and destroying forests and grasslands.

The economy and the culture of many native peoples has shifted from a sense of collective responsibility for community well-being based on shared public space and the common good to an individualistic ethic that focuses on self. Whereas in the past the community could be defined by how it shared the bounty of the land with itself and visitors, now it is disorientated and disconnected from the land and the customs that physically, environmentally, and morally sustained them.

Such changes in the perspective on the natural world have been both cause and effect of the loss of self-respect and concern for the environment that has affected us. So much that was based on values has been lost.

*

The Wounds

The question of why humans insist on laying waste to that which keeps us alive is perhaps unanswerable. It is based on behaviors that may have been suitable for us when we were fewer in number and could destroy vegetation and move on with relatively limited effect on the environment, but that now pose a threat to our very existence. Nonetheless, although we may not know *why* we act this way, it's essential that we address the attitudes that lead us to such self-destruction before it's too late.

Along with a shift in consciousness, there is a need for a change in 'perspective.' We need to reflect more thoughtfully on our responsibilities to the planet and to one another, and provide a way forward to heal all these wounds by embracing creation in all its diversity, beauty, and wonder. To do so, we need to take another look at planet Earth.

The Power of the Tree

The first value at the center of the Green Belt Movement's work is a demonstrable love for the environment. Such a love doesn't have to be sentimental, or imply that human beings should not utilize the resources in the natural environment. Many tree seedlings and full-grown trees die because of lack of care or drought. Or they have been cut for firewood or fencing, which may have been the original purpose for which they were grown. Such use is okay, as long as the land isn't left bare, and trees and forests aren't exploited carelessly or for the gain of only a few, while many suffer the loss of the ecological services (such as regulating rainfall or stopping erosion) that the trees and forests provide.

Even before the arrival of white settlers in the early 1900s, the countryside around the five forested mountains in Kenya was intensively cultivated and relatively densely populated. Nonetheless, the native peoples maintained extensive forest reserves where populations of elephants, leopards, buffaloes, and many other animals flourished. Although trees were cut down in these reserves and elsewhere, the communities made a habit of first using underbrush and already thinned forested areas to create houses and for firewood, leaving the larger, straighter trees to stand.

Such customs allowed the local communities to practice a form of agroforestry that retained water and topsoil. Each tree that was left standing was called in Kikuyu, for example, *mǒutilde; rema-kǒitilde;rǒitilde;ti*, or 'one that resists the cutting of the forest.' These trees were considered the habitation of the spirits of all the trees that had been cut down. In turn, the standing trees couldn't be felled unless the spirit was transferred to another tree. This was achieved by placing a stick against the tree to be cut down and then moving it to one that was to remain standing, or by planting another tree immediately in the same place as the felled one. Clearly, such restrictions stopped wholesale deforestation from taking place.

Many communities didn't revere trees per se, but the locals did choose certain species of trees and bushes at the base of which sacrifices were performed, both for their families and for the community at large. In Kikuyuland, one of these was the *m◠utilde;gumo* or fig tree (*Ficus natalensis*). Although not every fig tree was deemed worthy of veneration, Kikuyu priests performed sacrifices only where fig trees stood. Once a ceremony had been carried on around it, that fig tree and its location became sacred. My mother told me very clearly when I was a child that I was never to collect twigs for firewood from around the fig tree near our homestead since, she said, it was 'a tree of God' (*mũtĩ wa Ngai*).

Conceiving of the fig tree as *mũtĩ wa Ngai* had a kind of protoecological reasoning behind it. The tree's deep root system prevented landslides and allowed rainwater to travel from underground reservoirs to the surface in the streams and rivulets that then burst through the soil. Killing or harming every fig tree would, therefore, mean destabilizing the soil and making both the conservation of water and removing it from the ground more difficult. This logic was clearly how many peoples, who may have also used their trees as sources of medicine and food, survived in environments that were sometimes harsh.

For my mother, and the generations before her, the honoring of certain trees was part of a general reverence for nature. In the Kikuyu tradition, one was obliged to remove one's sandals if you approached a tree during a ceremony or were climbing Mount Kenya, which at the turn of the last century was completely covered with trees. Even those elders with spiritual authority would walk barefoot if they went up the mountain; indeed, so sacred was the mountain that it was impermissible to even crush wild mushrooms underfoot on one's journey through its forest.

*

Since the beginnings of human culture, the tree has been not only a source of food, medicine, and building material but a place of healing, consolation, and connection – with other human beings and with the divine. Trees are among the oldest, as well as largest, living organisms on the planet, so it's not surprising that human beings should have conceived of them in religious terms.[1] The Jewish mystical tradition kabalah depicts the connection between heaven and earth as an upside-down tree. The ancient Hindu texts known as the Upanishads mention the pipal (or *asvattha*) tree, which, with its roots in heaven and its canopy in the earth, is considered to be the manifestation of Brahma in the universe. In Norse mythology, the ash tree Yggdrasil is rooted in the underground and its branches support the home of the gods. Indeed, in my more fanciful moments I conceive of the tree as an upside-down person, with her head in the soil and her legs and feet in the air. The tree uses it roots to eat and its leaves to breathe, while the trunk resembles the human body.

Through the symbol of the *axis mundi* – the

cosmic pole around which everything is ordered – the tree has even embodied the universe itself. Ancient Egyptians believed that a great sycamore connected the worlds of life and death and that a huge tree arched over the earth and contained the sky beneath it. In a story echoed in Genesis, the ancient Babylonians conceived of two trees that guarded the eastern entry to heaven. For the peoples of northern Ghana, the baobab was the pathway by which human beings came down to earth from heaven. The Mayan civilization of Central America venerated the ceiba, which they called Yaxche, the Tree of Life; it supported the heavens. In its cosmology, the Zoroastrian tradition of Persia features the Saena, or the Tree of All Healing.

Certain species of trees have also been important spiritual centers. In southern Ghana, many communities continue to recognize as sacred the *Okoubaka aubrevillei*, *Milicia excelsa*, and a species of liana, while the Shona of Zimbabwe hold that ancestral spirits dwelled in the *mobola* plum tree. In areas of South Africa the *marula* is considered sacred. The Yoruba of West Africa believe that the iroko, cotton, baobab, and African sandalwood trees are the residences of a number of deities. Sacred groves exist in Nkoranza, Ghana, and throughout Malawi, while the grove dedicated to the *oshun*, or female goddesses, of the Yoruba near the town of Oshogbo in Nigeria is so important that the United Nations Educational, Scientific and Cultural Organization (UNESCO) has named it a World Heritage site. The Ndembu of Zambia, Congo, and Angola use the *mudyi* or milk tree for a number of cultural and sacred practices, as they do the *muyoomb* and *kapwiip*, which they call 'the elder of all trees.' Plants can be venerated even in those areas of Africa where there is less forest cover. For instance, the Tuareg of North Africa deem the *Maerua crassifolia* to be a place where spirits dwell.

The Hebrew scriptures similarly place an emphasis on trees – and not merely within the Garden of Eden – as a token of God's presence. After the flood, the dove returns with a leaf from an olive tree in its beak as a sign that Noah's ark can come to rest. The Israelite leader Joshua is believed to have established a pillar under an oak tree at which to honor Yahweh, and Abraham places his tents within sacred groves of trees in Shechem, Hebron, and Beersheba in order to be closer to God. The prophet Ezekiel conceives of God as a tree that produces water from its roots, while both Jeremiah and Hosea compare Israel to a tree. When the Israelites are forced into exile in Babylon, they famously hang their harps upon the willows, which thereafter became a symbol of mourning. In Asia, legend has it that the Buddha was born beneath a sal tree, and experienced his first deep meditative state under a rose apple before finding enlightenment underneath the bo or banyan, which thenceforth became known as the bodhi tree. In Japan, the oldest Shinto shrines are often to be found on hillsides or within groves of trees, and a religious frame of mind is one of the qualities that cultivating bonsai trees is intended to generate.

The ancient Germans considered the oak and spruce trees to be sacred, while the ancient

Greeks dedicated the laurel, olive, myrtle, ivy, and oak to Apollo, and the cypress to Hades. An oak formed the site of worship to Zeus at Dodona in Epirus, while the Romans linked the myrtle with Venus and Neptune. Plato's academy was situated in a grove of trees dedicated to Athena, the goddess of wisdom. Even today, the ancient Greek tradition of associating the olive branch with peace and the laurel wreath with achievement in competitive sports continues.

Pre-Christian Celtic lore also honored sacred forests. Some churches and cathedrals in Europe are decorated with the visage of the pre-Christian 'Green Man,' who was emblematic of spring and fertility, and often decorated with leaves. Within the Christian tradition, some trees play an important symbolic role. Palm leaves are strewn before Jesus as he enters Jerusalem, and the palm, cypress, myrtle, and olive all symbolize aspects of the Virgin Mary. The columns of Egyptian temples were shaped to reflect the stems of the lotus, palm, and papyrus trees, and Vitruvius, the first-century

B.C.E. Roman writer on architecture, suggested that the columns of Greek and Roman temples may themselves have been modeled on tree trunks. In all such places of worship, including Christian churches and cathedrals, the areas within the buildings' colonnades mimic the cool enclosure of an opening surrounded by tall trees, whose canopy provides protection from the elements and yet whose vaulting space gives a feeling of openness and uplift that encourages a sense of the divine.

In addition to the sacred grove – a space in the forest where the divine might be experienced – many religious traditions honor the individual retiring into more intimate or stark landscapes to receive divine messages. The undulating landscape of the Central Highlands of Kenya provided many places for Kikuyu priests to escape and commune with God or to receive inspiration. Kikuyu lore has it that the Kikuyu traditions and language, which is rich with sayings and idioms, and through which efforts were made to create a form of writing, were developed between harvests in the many caves in the region by *aini a gĕ̃itilde;chandĕ̃itilde;* ('players of the *gĕ̃itilde;chandĕ̃itilde;,*' an instrument made from a gourd). These grottos might be near waterfalls or rivers; they would be naturally covered by vegetation and thus it would be easy to secrete oneself away.

The Archangel Gabriel is thought to have given the Prophet Muhammad the Qur'an in a cave. The Hebrew prophet Elijah flees into the countryside, and hides near a brook where he is fed by ravens. The Mormon religion began when Joseph Smith received his revelations in a sacred grove in Palmyra, New York. John the Baptist, of course, prophesies the coming of the Messiah in the wilderness, and Jesus goes into the desert in order to be tested. Through the course of the three years of his ministry, Jesus retreats several times to be alone (for instance, Luke 6:12). On the last night of his freedom, he removes himself to pray in the Garden of Gethsemane. Even cathedrals and churches – which encourage such lofty senses of the divine – provide chapels where one can be alone with one's thoughts and one's God.

Because of their spiritual resonance, as well as the shade and space they offer, trees provide natural focal points for a community to come together to deliberate its future or for elders to render judgments on contentious issues. Consequently, it's not surprising that certain trees became symbols of a group's identity. I encountered this firsthand in 2006 in the Basque region of northern Spain, where the local government was partnering with the Green Belt Movement to plant trees and offset greenhouse gas emissions. Representatives of the administration took me to see an oak tree that marked the site of the original Basque government. The oak, which was about twenty years old, was said to be the fourth tree that had been planted on that site since the fourteenth century.

The Basque people are not alone in considering a tree the locus of judgment and government. In Kenya, Samburu leaders traditionally gather under a tree to discuss issues. The early Israelite judge Deborah takes her seat under the palm tree to exercise her wisdom. The Oromo of Ethiopia and Kenya deem the scepter tree (also known as the *bokku*) a suitable place for officials of the traditional courts to gather. The judges from the Maasai and Kalenjin communities traditionally sat under a tree, and once ensconced beneath it one was obliged to tell the truth – much as placing one's hand on the Bible is meant to encourage honesty in a court of law today. In addition to providing shade for learning and government in Southeast Asia, and Java in particular, the banyan has also been used as a place under which to conduct business in Gujarat, India.[2] The early Buddhist *sanghas* likewise practiced their austerities within the forest.

Among Kikuyus, once men had finished raising their children, they were expected to become guardians of wisdom and protectors of the community's way of life. As such, they were considered peacemakers and judges, and during the ceremony inducting them into elderhood they were given a staff from the *thügeĩ* tree. This mark of authority allowed them to officiate in the various ceremonies and rituals that marked the communities' rites of passage and sacrifices.

When he was about to perform a ceremony, a Kikuyu elder would disappear to a special, sacred location in the forest for seven days to purify himself. The number seven signified a bad omen for Kikuyus, so staying in the forest for a week meant that the omen could be reversed. During this time, the elder would take no alcohol, and refrain from sexual activity and other pleasures. He would try to rid himself of bad thoughts and focus on the ceremony at hand: why it needed to be performed and the meaning of its practice. The ceremonies themselves were attempts to appease God, who would have precipitated whatever the community was facing: a drought, a famine, barrenness, or an epidemic of disease.

Whenever a judgment was to be made, the *thiig&itilde*; stick had to be present; it was the signal that violence was unacceptable. I recall my mother telling me that if there was a dispute between men from different mountain ridges, the elders from the opposing groups would meet. If they decided there was to be no conflict, rather than announcing their judgment directly to the young fighters, the elders would stand on their side of the riverbank and stretch their *thiig&itilde*; staffs so that they pointed toward one another. The elders would then declare a truce by saying in unison, *mbaara horoho*, or 'let the conflict end.' Once the elders uttered those words, the warriors would depart without speaking or showing any aggression to the other side. This ritual was as binding as a signed peace treaty, and it served very well to maintain peace within and between the communities.

It needs to be reiterated that honoring and sacramentalizing trees in these communities didn't mean that they could never be cut down or utilized for ordinary purposes. In fact, they always have been, even to make sacred spaces. The temple built by Solomon is made from oak, palm, date, and willow trees, among other natural elements. Hindu temples are often constructed of wood from the deodar.

Within the broader perspective of public policy,

therefore, if trees have been grown only for timber, then it seems reasonable to cut them in their prime and use the wood. What needs to be borne in mind, however, is that the conventional economics of natural-resource use – that a tree is only as valuable as the amount of money that can be obtained for the products that can be made from it – fail to account for the many other values that human beings draw from the world around them. In fact, scientists are only now beginning to understand the vast range of services – natural, social, psychological, ecological, and economic – that forests perform: the water they clean and retain; the climate patterns they regulate; the medicines they contain; the food they supply; the soil they enrich; the carbon they entrap; the oxygen they emit; the species of flora and fauna they conserve; and the peoples whose very physical existence depends on them.

In 1997, a coalition of scientists estimated that the total dollar value of the planet's ecosystemic services was $33 trillion – or almost double the then gross national product of the United States ($18 trillion).[3] On a local level, these services can be of crucial significance. For instance, planting and ensuring the survival of 30,000 acres (12,000 hectares) of mangrove trees in Vietnam cost $1 million, but saved $7 million a year in maintenance costs for the country's dykes, according to a recent report from the United Nations Environment Programme. While shrimp farms, which often require clearing coastal mangroves, can generate (with subsidies) up to $1,220 a hectare (2.5 acres), the losses to local communities of wood and nonwood forest products, fishing, and coastal protection adds up to nearly ten times that: $12,000 a hectare. And after five years of commercial shrimp farming, when the environment is exhausted and the operations move on, restoration costs are estimated at $9,000 a hectare.[4]

That some rare tropical hardwoods are made into such functional items as boardwalks, benches, or even chopsticks – and that so much goes to waste – suggests just how far removed we are from understanding the power and value of trees and forests, and of loving the environment.

When we reflect on the sacred groves and the spiritual and symbolic weight we have given to trees and forests, it seems self-evident that not only have trees been our constant companions, but we would quite literally not be human if we didn't perhaps feel regret when a tree disappears from the landscape. For when it does, a fundamental concept from the Garden of Eden also disappears.

It is possible to live within a forest and not really *see* it, or dwell in the countryside and not appreciate and be inspired by the nature that surrounds you. The prophet Jeremiah laments those 'who have eyes, but do not see, who have ears, but do not hear' (Jer. 5:21). When I raise the issue of the loss of the natural world in the Green Belt Movement's civic and environmental seminars, many participants tell me that it's as if they had looked at the world around them for the first time. 'Until I took this course,' one representative woman said, 'I didn't see the bare fields and roadsides or the denuded landscapes. Now I see areas where there should be trees, and rivers filled with silt that I hadn't noticed before.' She finally *saw* what had been in front of her all along; her consciousness had been raised, and now she was in a position to participate in the process of healing.

Perhaps this is why, as I watched that two-hundred-year-old sapele fall to the ground that day in the Congo, it felt to me as though something extraordinarily weighty and consequential had been brought low. In its collapse was an echo of the trees and whole forests disappearing all over the world. Perhaps, too, given the age of the tree, I'd recognized something of myself in it: in the passage of our many years, we had turned from limber youth to creaking old age, our fresh limbs knotted and worn by time, yet still, I hope, with a contribution to make and still holding on to our lives with an element of dignity and resilience.

I could imagine how far that tree had come, from its beginnings as a tiny seed one could hold in one's hand to a mighty organism that had outlived many generations of humans. Such a journey – nurtured in the darkness of the soil, the lightness of the sun, and the dampness of water – could be explained by science, but somehow it was still miraculous: that life of such grandeur and permanence could have emerged from something so small and fragile. The spread of the roots downward and the branches upward provided a glimpse of the beauty and complexity of natural processes that our scientific instruments, for all their sophistication, still aren't quite able to explicate.

That more than half of the wood from the tree would go up in smoke – even though it had until the moment it was cut down possessed a hardiness that enabled it to withstand storms, soak up the rain, and hold fast during dry spells – also upset me. Its branches had hosted insects of various sorts, and, despite the risk of loss of a limb or two, and the parasites and birds that may have bored holes into its trunk or eaten out its inside, it had continued to grow. But now the tree was no more because it had been judged to have greater value dead than alive.

*

One aspect of a love of nature that we need to foster is experiential. Nature – and in particular, the wild – feeds our spirit, and a direct encounter with it is vital in helping us appreciate and care for it. For unless we see it, smell it, or touch it, we tend to forget it, and our souls wither. This is particularly true in urban settings or industrialized countries where direct experience of the untamed is less common, and it's the main reason so many tourists visit Kenya (for the most part, they're not coming to see the Kenyan people!). They want to see the large animals in their natural habitat. Many develop a connection to a lion or an elephant or a wildebeest, and they want to help keep them alive.

In many ways, this search for the wild is an attempt to heal the 'dis-ease' we all live with, since none of us is immune to the effects of environmental degradation or diminishment of the natural world. I feel it when I'm in the countryside in Kenya and see bare hillsides and rivers red with silt, which harms both people and other species. Likewise, I feel ease when I visit places where trees, particularly those planted by Green Belt Movement groups, have grown and cover a swath of green land that was once bare.

I remember on one occasion we visited a site that had been used for cash crops and then, when the soil was exhausted, abandoned. Through our efforts, the grasses and small bushes that formed the undergrowth out of which native trees could grow had returned, and vegetation covered the ground so completely that one would have been forgiven for thinking that agriculture had never taken place there. Near the site, we came across two streams, which a local forester told us had sprung up since the rehabilitation of the woodland. As we descended into a deep valley, we could see the water from the streams merging with the river, which had deepened and become enlivened. Seeing the replenishment of the deforested area and the resurgent streams almost overwhelmed me. Not only was the land recovering, but we had been instrumental in creating water where none had existed for years. It seemed like a miracle from God – like

Moses striking the rock and seeing water gushing forth into the desert (see Num. 20:11)!

I'm sure I'm not alone in feeling my heart stir when I see rivers cleared of silt as forests are replanted with indigenous trees, or when I meet someone who says his life was changed by the work we have done. When we experience something pleasant, such as standing in a forest listening to the birds, the insects, and the sound of the wind in the branches, we are filled with a sense of well-being. It's as if what we're searching for finally has been found.

Certainly it's important to read about the earth, and understanding its systems also helps create a connection to it, and a desire to want to do something for it. However, if you detach yourself completely from the reality of nature, you lose a little of the knowledge about what is happening to the planet. It is worth remembering that for the last fifty years, scientists working with the soil, in the forests, and in the oceans have told the rest of the world of the mounting evidence of drastic changes to the earth because of toxic pollutants, habitat loss, species extinction, depletion of the ozone layer, and changes in climate and temperature from the greenhouse effect, which we know today as global warming. They gathered data, but they did so *within* the natural environment. This is also why I believe it's so essential to have environmental education in schools that includes experiential learning, so children can touch the soil and see the worms, or tend a garden and harvest and eat what they grow. Unfortunately, if they don't have such experiences, or if they never plant a tree, they may not know what they have missed until it's too late. They may never rediscover the lost sacred groves.

Sacred Groves, Sacred No More

Through the centuries, as worldviews have collided, trees, because of their resonance and power to human beings, have become, literally, totems of the clashes between different groups. Whether trees have been understood by their communities as nodal points that connect the world above with the world below, or as places where one's ancestors and/or their spirits reside, invading forces have understood that sacred groves or trees must not only be destroyed, but that such destruction is an extremely potent way to demoralize, fragment, and intimidate the local population by stripping it of both its economic and its spiritual sources and strengths.

As many fairy tales attest, the woods can inspire fear as places of transformation where the ordered world is subjected to the disorders of Nature. The forest is where Hansel and Gretel meet the witch; Snow White flees into the woods to escape her wicked stepmother; the thorns and thickets of a hundred years have to be cut through if the prince is to rescue Sleeping Beauty; and it is in the woods where Little Red Riding Hood encounters the wolf.

Of course, these ideas say more about the social identities of the various societies and cultures that hold these concepts than they do about trees per se. For many native peoples, such as the Aka of the Congo and other forest dwellers, the forests have not been fearful places that they must conquer or where they cannot go, but their entire *world*, the source for their food and medicine, clothing and shelter. To the Aka, the forest – and indeed what the world calls the 'environment' – does not exist beyond or outside the human realm. In other words, Nature is not something set apart, with or against which we react. It's not a place we fear as something within which we might lose our humanity or, conversely, a place where we might gain perspective and simplicity away from the corruption and treachery of the court or the city. It is, instead, something within which human beings are enfolded.

This battle for control over the meaning of the spiritual landscape is an ancient one. An example of such a conflict can be found in the Hebrew scriptures, with the struggle of the Yahwistic priests to destroy the cult of Asherah, a goddess who in her various forms the Israelites came across once they settled in Canaan, and who was worshipped extensively during the first and second millennia before the common era. The most common form of reverence – as the writers of the books of Kings, Chronicles, Isaiah, and Jeremiah note – consisted of worshippers building 'for themselves high places, pillars, and sacred poles [*asherim*] on every high hill and under every green tree' (see 1 Kings 14:23; 2 Kings 17:10, et passim). Of the twenty-two references to *asherim* in the Hebrew Bible, most involve either the condemnation of kings or groups who set them up or the praising of those in authority who tear them down.

Scholars have traditionally called Asherah a fertility goddess, although such a designation has been questioned.[1] In the Kikuyu tradition, women who were unable to conceive would carry dolls on their backs and visit a fig tree, where the local holy man would conduct a ceremony. In much the same way as the maypole in Europe, the totem in various Native American cultures, and the lingams and stupas of south Asian cultures, offer connections between the tree as a symbol of power and a phallic object suggesting fertility, so the *asherim* may have been a sign of the ever-recurring potency of the tree, which constantly renews life, year after year.

The religious and political authorities of ancient Israel clearly considered that worship of the *asherim* was against Yahweh's commandment and tore down the sacred sites. Following a similar approach, saints Benedict and Boniface in the sixth and seventh centuries, as well as Charlemagne in the eighth, destroyed pre-Christian groves in Europe, not only to prove that the powers contained within the trees or groves were idolatrous and therefore no match for the Christian God but to force the locals to convert to the new faith.

Such acts of sacred vandalism for religious and political purposes are not confined to the ancient past. From the moment they set foot on foreign shores, colonial forces demonized and marginalized the religious practices of those they conquered and occupied. As with the followers of Asherah, the Kikuyus were told that God could not be worshipped outdoors, in the high places or in the forests, but that he was to be found only in the building built for him, where an altar would be set up and controlled by a priest whose authority had come not from the community but from another representative who lived many miles away.

On August 4, 1914, the British burned and destroyed the houses and sacred groves that belonged to the Giriama, a community whose ancestral home was along the coast of Kenya. Their objective was to stamp out resistance to the program of taxation and recruitment to the workforce the colonial authority intended to impose. This occurred on the same day that

Britain declared war on Germany, in a global conflict that would leave millions dead among the destroyed homes, mud, and shattered tree stumps of the battlefields.

Even today, communities know that destruction of sacred trees carries a potent message. In January 2002, a minister belonging to the Assemblies of God church in Laikipia district, on the northern side of Mount Kenya, gathered members of his congregation to cut down and burn a sacred fig tree. Called *oroteti*, it was where elders had prayed and made offerings during several years of drought. On many occasions, the government of Kenya has barred some members of the Kikuyu community from praying to God facing Mount Kenya, or visiting the mountain on a spiritual pilgrimage, because such practices are deemed unacceptable by the dominant form of Christianity.

Just as invading forces know that cutting down sacred groves and trees can assist in quelling a community's recalcitrance, so resistance to the imposition of different social or religious customs, or economic agendas, has sometimes taken the form of communities rallying to protect trees. One could also see such actions as demonstrating a love for the environment.

One of the best known is from the 1970s, when rural men and women in the Indian Himalayas became distressed by the destruction logging companies were causing to their forests. The Chipko movement, as the informal groups were called (from the Hindi word meaning 'to embrace'), adopted the nonviolent resistance techniques of *satyagraha* (or 'truth-power'), as Mahatma Gandhi named it. Risking major injury, the peasants joined their hands around trees in order to stop them from being felled. The modern Chipko movement was inspired by a 'chipko' incident from the eighteenth century, when three hundred people in the village of Kherjarli in northwest India died hugging *khejri* trees, seeking to protect them from loggers dispatched by the local ruler.[2]

When I first started the Green Belt Movement, I didn't know about either the modern or the historical Chipko movements, but I quickly learned about them. In 1981, their leaders participated in a United Nations' conference on new and renewable sources of energy, which took place in Kenya. Many of us, including members of the Chipko and Green Belt movements, marched together through the streets of Nairobi to advocate that planting trees was creating renewable energy and providing firewood. Almost thirty years later, the world gathered in Copenhagen, Denmark, at a United Nations' climate summit, to discuss whether avoiding deforestation and the degradation of forests, thereby protecting intact forests, would be one of the solutions to global warming.

One of the supporters of the Chipko acts of resistance in the early 1970s was the physicist and social activist Vandana Shiva, whose organization Navdanya is currently fighting to save biodiversity and the livelihoods and seed stocks of Indian farmers. Also in the Chipko tradition are the many people behind Narmada Bachao Andolan, a collection of organizations that protested the building of the dam over the Narmada River in Gujarat. Echoes of the Chipko movement's inspiration continue to this day in the Appiko movement (which means 'embrace' in Kannada, the major language of Karnataka state in southern India), and with women in Himachal Pradesh in the very north of India. In 2009, they tied sacred threads, or *rakhis*, which symbolize the bond between a sister and a brother, around trees slated to be engulfed if the Renuka dam was built.[3] (Such an activism based on values founded on faith inspires me. Whenever I am in the Indian subcontinent, I am very aware of the great spiritual traditions of the land – including Hinduism, Buddhism, Jainism, Sikhism, and Islam.)

Two of the Chipko movement's principal figures, Sunderlal Bahuguna and Indu Tikekar, pointed out when they accepted the Right Livelihood Award on behalf of the movement in December 1987 that what started as an economic campaign to protect the forest as 'a source of employment through tree-felling and providing raw material for industries' became something more – an act of resistance based on acknowledgment that the services that the forests provide are at once economic *and* spiritual:

The long sufferings of hill-women have guided the activists to reach new heights in their movement, when these persevering mothers of the future generations dictated that forests were their maternal homes, which provided water, food, fodder, and fuel. Both the trees and the mothers teach that to live and also to be ready to die for the sake of others proves to be the real fountain of bliss. Thus came the famous slogan:

What do the forests bear?

Soil, water, and pure air;

Soil, water, and pure air

Are the basis of life.[4]

Another act of resistance in the Chipko spirit occurred in 1997, when a twenty-three-year-old American, Julia Butterfly Hill, climbed an ancient redwood tree she called Luna in Northern California that was about to be logged. She lived on a tiny platform in a tent within Luna's branches for more than two years – through hot weather and cold, rain-storms, snowfall, and even a hurricane – as a protest against the cutting of these majestic trees, many of which were hundreds of years old. Her tree-sit generated tremendous media interest and brought the issue of the protection of old-growth forest in California to national and international attention. Eventually, Luna and some other redwood trees were saved, and Julia came down. (She admits she didn't plan to spend two years almost two hundred feet from the ground, and, indeed, the group that was organizing the protest against the lumber company was perhaps even more surprised than she was at the length of her stay.)

I feel kinship with Julia, not only because she saw the beauty of a tree and decided to do something to protect it and express her love for the environment, but because she recognized a wrong being done and decided to try to stop it.

While Julia was in the tree, she developed a close fellowship with it:

Perched above everything and peering down, I
felt as if I was standing on nothing at all, even
though this massive, solid tree rose underneath me. I held on with my legs and reached
my hands into the heavens. My feet could feel
the power of the earth coming through Luna,
while my hands felt the power of the sky. It
was magical. I felt perfectly balanced. I was
one with Creation.[5]

During the storms to which Julia was subjected,
she found herself bending and swaying along
with the branches as they tossed in the wind
and rain. The tree, of course, was also helping
sustain Julia by providing her with oxygen to
breathe even as she was providing it, as she
breathed out, with the carbon dioxide it needed.

To some, of course, assigning a name, a spiritual dimension, or distinctiveness to trees may
seem absurd; something suitable for poets and
primitives, perhaps, but not a rational or scientific response to the biological cycles of decay
and regeneration that have neither personality
nor moral compass. Indeed, it may be pointed

out that the natural world, for all its symbioses and ecological harmonies, is also one of a pitiless struggle to survive, of parasites and predators, extinctions and disease. The forests are merely one natural resource among many; our only responsibility is to use them wisely.

But the beauty of Julia's gesture was that she didn't balk at the naysayers who looked at the tree and said, in effect, there are millions of other trees in forests across the world that are being logged and that it was useless to try to save one tree or the grove that surrounded it. She didn't rationalize her gesture against the likely outcome. She simply climbed the tree, and slowly, the derision her act had received from many quarters changed to a grudging admiration; the issue of clear-cutting in the Pacific Northwest was no longer ignored; and the pressure to come to an arrangement whereby Luna might be saved (an arrangement that hadn't existed before) became too much for the forces arrayed against her to resist. Julia's act demonstrated not only a positive value but how much we've lost. That sense of beauty, awe, and harmony in nature has too often given way to another vision of what we can use, exploit, and control.

This attitude has extended to all of nature. When, for example, I look back on the Kikuyu way of life that existed before colonialism, I am sure that one of the reasons the community appeared to have so much time to celebrate and enjoy the natural world was because they weren't looking at it through acquisitive, materialistic eyes. To take just one example: They didn't go to a river trying to figure out how they could privatize the water, put it in a bottle, and sell it; they relaxed and appreciated its beauty, grew arrowroots or bananas or sugarcane along its banks, and marveled at the fish that swim in it.

If we love the environment, we must identify with the tree that is cut down, and the human and other communities that are dying because their land no longer sustains them. We must express regrets for the destroyed landscapes, become angry when we hear of another species under threat from human activity or see another polluted river or a landfill. We need to honor our hunger for beauty amid the sterility of an urban environment with no parks or trees or flowers. We need to recognize the despair we may feel when a river no longer reaches the sea, or a lake's bottom is caked with cracked mud.

What if those of us who live in environments that are threatened decided that we'd only use trees that fell and died because of weather events, disease, or age? Or that we'd only use those trees that were not essential to protect water supplies or to sustain biodiversity? We might be very challenged, of course, to continue our accumulation of goods and the improvement of quality of life that we value in monetary terms. On the other hand, we may start to replenish the stocks of water, reduce the effect of global greenhouse emissions, stop soil erosion, bring back endangered species, and support a host of other life-affirming services that we have not monetized because we assume they aren't economically important – unless we can use them in commercial activities. We might also recognize that we have a host of new friends with which to commune – the trees whose lives we spared, and that breathe in symbiosis with us. We might reduce our competition with other people over access to those trees and cultivate cultures of peace with our neighbors.

This can be done. The Green Belt Movement and the Kenyan army held civic and environment education seminars, for instance, that led to an unprecedented action. The army, whose soldiers have been trained to protect our territory against an invasion by an outside enemy, recognized that unless we take care of our water, forests, and land, not only will we Kenyans be likely to fight among ourselves for access to those resources, but the country itself will be threatened with desertification. Under the leadership of the army's chief of general staff, General Jeremiah Kianga, the Kenyan army began a campaign to protect seedlings and plant trees in their barracks, as well as inside national forests. The soldiers were quick to understand that the encroaching desert under their feet is as dangerous as a foreigner wielding a weapon who claims a part of Kenya.

The spreading of the Sahara southward and

the Kalahari north is not an idle concern. As trees are cut and planting stops, even the grasses eventually vanish. The animals disappear and all that is left is sand. People are then forced to migrate and move toward areas already settled by other communities. This is already happening in places such as Darfur, in Sudan, as well as in Kenya, where struggles over land and water are politicized and often characterized as age-old tribal rivalries. Why should we be surprised that in such situations, conflict becomes more likely, and we ourselves become a little coarser, harder, more easily moved to violence because we have been cut off from that which gives us life? For we are neglecting a threat not only to our national borders but to the future of civilization. While this threat doesn't carry a gun or a bomb, it is stealthy, and over the long term it promises to be just as devastating. No weapons will counteract this threat. Only a change of consciousness that includes rediscovering that love of nature that animated the minds and souls of our ancestors can. This is when sacred groves become sacred again.

Notes

The Power of the Tree

1. Information about the social and religious uses of the tree is referenced from many articles in the *Encyclopedia of Religion and Nature*, edited by Bron Taylor (New York: Continuum, 2005). Also included is information from *The Encyclopedia of Religion*, Second Edition, edited by Lindsay Jones (Farmington Hills, Mich.: Macmillan), pp. 9333–40. Also sourced are *The Oxford Handbook of Religion and Ecology*, edited by Roger S. Gottlieb (New York: Oxford University Press, 2006), and *This Sacred Earth: Religion, Nature, Environment*, edited by Roger S. Gottlieb (New York: Routledge, 1996).

2. 'In the Shade of the Banyan Tree,' *The Economist*, April 8, 2009.

3. Robert Costanza, et al. 'The Value of the World's Ecosystem Services and Natural Capital,' sourced

from the website of the University of Vermont's Gund Institute for Ecological Economics, www. uvm.edu/giee/publications/Nature_Paper.pdf.

4. UN Environment Programme, *TEEB – The Economics of Ecosystems and Biodiversity [TEEB] for National and International Policy Makers – Summary: Responding to the Value of Nature,* 2009, and press release, 'TEEB report released on the Economics of Ecosystems and Biodiversity for National and International Policy Makers,' November 13, 2009.

Sacred Groves, Sacred No More

1. Christine Downing, *The Goddess: Mythological Images of the Feminine* (New York: Crossroad Publishing Company, 1981), pp. 13–16; Steve Davis, 'The Canaanite-Hebrew Goddess,' in *The Book of the Goddess Past and Present,* Carl Olson, ed. (New York: Crossroad Publishing Company, 1992), pp. 68–79; Susan Ackerman, 'Asherah/Asherim' in The Jewish Women's Archive, http://jwa.org/encyclopedia/article/asherahasherim-bible; David Leeming, *Jealous Gods & Chosen People: The Mythology of the Middle East* (New York: Oxford University Press, 2004), p. 94.

Notes

2. Information about the Chipko movement gathered from Wikipedia, http://en.wikipedia.org/wiki/Chipko_movement.

3. Himachal Pradesh, IANS, 'New Chipko Movement: Himachal Women Tie Rakhis to Protect Trees,' *Deccan Herald*, August 3, 2009.

4. The speech can be read in its entirety at www.rightlivelihood.org/chipko_speech.html.

5. Julia Butterfly Hill, *The Legacy of Luna: The Story of a Tree, a Woman and the Struggle to Save the Redwoods* (San Francisco: HarperOne, 2001), p. 123.